Pfeiffer™

Coaching for Commitment

COACHING SKILLS INVENTORY (CSI): SELF

THIRD EDITION

Cindy Coe

Amy Zehnder

Dennis Kinlaw

John Wiley & Sons, Inc.

Published by Pfeiffer
An Imprint of Wiley
989 Market Street, San Francisco, CA 94103-1741
www.pfeiffer.com

For additional copies/bulk purchases of this book in the U.S. please contact 800-274-4434.

Pfeiffer books and products are available through most bookstores. To contact Pfeiffer directly call our Customer Care Department within the U.S. at 800-274-4434, outside the U.S. at 317-572-3985, fax 317-572-4002, or visit www.pfeiffer.com.

Pfeiffer also publishes its books in a variety of electronic formats. Some content that appears in print may not be available in electronic books.

ISBN: 978-0-7879-8253-9
Acquiring Editor: Martin Delahoussaye
Director of Development: Kathleen Dolan Davies
Developmental Editor: Susan Rachmeler
Production Editor: Dawn Kilgore
Editor: Rebecca Taff
Editorial Assistant: Julie Rodriquez
Manufacturing Supervisor: Becky Morgan

Printed in the United States of America

Printing 10 9 8 7 6 5 4 3 2 1

Coaching Skills Inventory (CSI): Self

Date: _____ Organization: _____

Name: _____

Job Title/Position: _____ Gender: M   F

Audience

The *Coaching Skills Inventory (CSI): Self* is intended for use by *anyone* who wants to identify (1) a coaching gap compared to an ideal, (2) the role(s) he or she gravitates toward, and (3) proficiency levels in using certain coaching skills during interactions with others.

Definitions

Each set of statements is preceded by a stem that includes the terms "colleagues and co-workers." Colleagues and co-workers are defined as anyone you have an interaction with, including team members, direct reports, supervisors, bosses, peers, students, and partners.

Instructions

For each item, indicate the degree to which you believe the skill or behavior is characteristic of your actions by circling the appropriate number on the scale. That is, if you believe the description is "very characteristic" of your own behavior, circle "5"; if it is "very uncharacteristic" of your own behavior, circle "1"; if your assessment lies somewhere in between these extremes, circle 2, 3, or 4, as appropriate.

Complete every item. Then follow the detailed instructions in the scoring section.

Take the Inventory

Decide to what degree each of the following statements is characteristic of your actions or behaviors in your day-to-day interactions and conversations with colleagues and co-workers. Circle the number that best represents you.

5	4	3	2	1
Very Characteristic	Moderately Characteristic	Somewhat Characteristic	Moderately Uncharacteristic	Very Uncharacteristic

When discussing issues with my colleagues and co-workers, I

1. Seek first to understand by soliciting more information. 　　5　4　3　2　1

2. Request others' opinions far more than I give my own. 　　5　4　3　2　1

3. Help others gain a full understanding of their own issues before moving forward. 　　5　4　3　2　1

4. Help others find their own solutions to problems. 　　5　4　3　2　1

5. Help others clarify their own feelings about issues. 　　5　4　3　2　1

6. Help others discover alternative solutions. 　　5　4　3　2　1

7. Help others test new ideas. 　　5　4　3　2　1

8. Help others take their share of responsibility for solving problems. 　　5　4　3　2　1

9. Help structure problem-solving conversations so that they move forward logically. 　　5　4　3　2　1

10. Help others identify the resources they need to solve problems. 　　5　4　3　2　1

11. Challenge the status quo by making truthful, non-judgmental statements to illuminate blind spots. 　　5　4　3　2　1

12. Make requests that stretch others' potential. 　　5　4　3　2　1

13. Use silence to gather more of the story. 　　5　4　3　2　1

14. Listen without taking over the conversation. 　　5　4　3　2　1

Whenever I have the chance, I help my colleagues and co-workers

15. Understand the political issues that must be taken into account in making decisions. 　　5　4　3　2　1

5	4	3	2	1
Very Characteristic	Moderately Characteristic	Somewhat Characteristic	Moderately Uncharacteristic	Very Uncharacteristic

Whenever I have the chance, I help my colleagues and co-workers

16. Understand the organizational history behind issues and problems.   5 4 3 2 1
17. Identify key players to consider in gaining acceptance of new ideas.   5 4 3 2 1
18. Become sensitive to those organizational values that can affect success.   5 4 3 2 1
19. Develop a personal network for growth opportunities.   5 4 3 2 1
20. Clarify career goals.   5 4 3 2 1
21. Understand their roles in achieving the organization's goals.   5 4 3 2 1
22. Become sensitive to the likes and dislikes of senior leaders.   5 4 3 2 1
23. Gain visibility in the larger organization.   5 4 3 2 1
24. Learn from their mistakes.   5 4 3 2 1

Whenever I have the chance with my colleagues and co-workers, I

25. Help them identify new learning opportunities.   5 4 3 2 1
26. Help them gain expert status in their current areas of responsibility.   5 4 3 2 1
27. Help them with new tasks they are learning to perform.   5 4 3 2 1
28. Help them analyze what knowledge and skills they need to succeed in their jobs.   5 4 3 2 1
29. Help them understand what needs to be done and how to accomplish it.   5 4 3 2 1
30. Encourage them to learn by teaching others.   5 4 3 2 1
31. Praise them when they have acquired some new knowledge or skills.   5 4 3 2 1
32. Demonstrate how much I value new learning.   5 4 3 2 1
33. Help them to find ways to reinforce their learning.   5 4 3 2 1

5	4	3	2	1
Very Characteristic	Moderately Characteristic	Somewhat Characteristic	Moderately Uncharacteristic	Very Uncharacteristic

Whenever I have the chance with my colleagues and co-workers, I

34. Serve as a resource in my areas of competence. 5 4 3 2 1

35. Acknowledge their efforts, accomplishments, struggles, and feelings. 5 4 3 2 1

36. Encourage them to come up with innovative solutions. 5 4 3 2 1

37. Ask questions based on others' needs, not my ideas or solutions. 5 4 3 2 1

38. Ask questions that encourage a deeper exploration. 5 4 3 2 1

When attempting to influence the performance of my colleagues and co-workers, I

39. Keep the performance expectations of self and others clear. 5 4 3 2 1

40. Promptly identify performance problems as they occur. 5 4 3 2 1

41. Gain commitment from others for continuous improvement and performance. 5 4 3 2 1

42. Confront performance problems in a way that maintains positive relationships. 5 4 3 2 1

43. Am concrete and specific in talking about performance problems. 5 4 3 2 1

44. Emphasize improvement in the future, rather than failure in the past. 5 4 3 2 1

45. Help others find their own best ways to improve their performance. 5 4 3 2 1

46. Encourage others to develop strategies for solving performance problems. 5 4 3 2 1

47. Challenge others to take on more and more difficult tasks. 5 4 3 2 1

48. Develop commitment to continuous improvement. 5 4 3 2 1

49. Ask them to pinpoint key areas of focus. 5 4 3 2 1

50. Keep the conversation focused on them and their accountabilities. 5 4 3 2 1

Scoring the CSI

IN THE COACHING WORLD, you must first know where you are in order to get where you want to be. The insight you gather through the use this inventory is designed to provide you with a clear picture of where you want to go.

Step 1. Total Your Scores

Fill in your totals by adding up the numeric value of the numbers you circled for each of the following groups of questions:

Pay close attention to the item numbers; they are not all sequential.

Roles

Total your scores for items *1 through 10*.   Enter total here: _____ = Coach

Total your scores for items *15 through 24*.   Enter total here: _____ = Mentor

Total your scores for items *25 through 34*.   Enter total here: _____ = Instructor

Total your scores for items *39 through 48*.   Enter total here: _____ = Manager

Highest possible score in any role = 50   *Lowest possible score in any role = 10*

CLEAR Coaching Skills

Total your scores for items *11 and 12*.   Enter total here: _____ = Challenge

Total your scores for items *13 and 14*.   Enter total here: _____ = Listen

Total your scores for items *35 and 36*.   Enter total here: _____ = Encourage

Total your scores for items *37 and 38*.   Enter total here: _____ = Ask

Total your scores for items *49 and 50*.   Enter total here: _____ = Refine

Transfer your scores to the corresponding roles (manager, mentor, instructor, coach) within the graphic. Watch carefully where you put your scores: Coach is at the bottom; Manager is upper-left; Instructor is upper-middle; and Mentor is upper-right.

For each role, find where your score would be on the diagram and draw a horizontal line representing your score. Shade in the section from the center point, the narrowest point of the hourglass shape (10), out to your score. An example is provided on the following page.

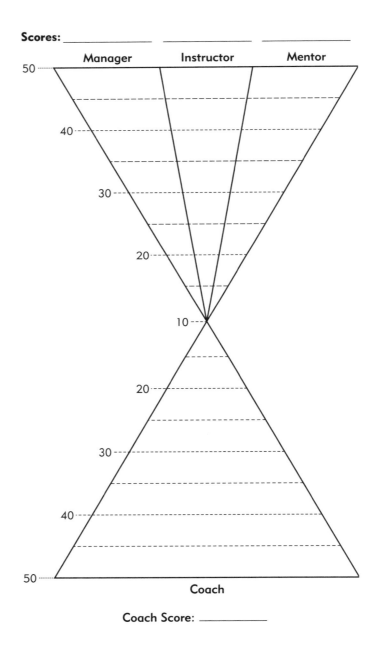

Scores: _____ _____ _____

Coach Score: _____

Scoring Example

Total scores for questions 1 through 10.   Enter total here: __15__   Coach

Total scores for questions 15 through 24.   Enter total here: __22__   Mentor

Total scores for questions 25 through 34.   Enter total here: __46__   Instructor

Total scores for questions 39 through 48.   Enter total here: __31__   Manager

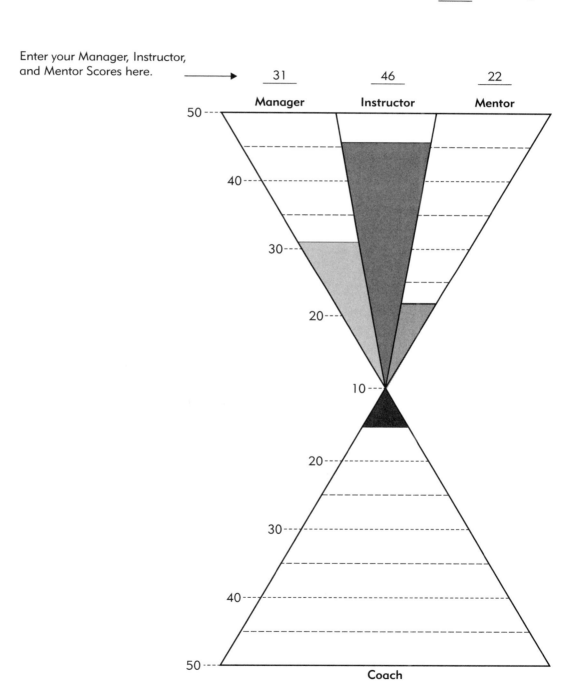

Enter your Manager, Instructor, and Mentor Scores here. →

Enter your Coach score here: __15__

Transfer your Coach score from Step 1 to the space provided below. Subtract your score from 50. The difference is your Coaching Gap.

$$\underset{\text{(minus)}}{\textbf{50}} \quad - \quad \underset{\text{Coach Score}}{\rule{3cm}{0.4pt}} \quad = \quad \underset{\text{My Coaching Gap}}{\rule{3cm}{0.4pt}}$$

To check your math; your number should be between 0 and 40.
The larger the score, the larger the coaching gap and the harder it will be for you to make the shift to the *coach role*.
The smaller the score, the smaller the coaching gap and the easier it will be for you to make the shift to the *coach role*.

Step 4. CLEAR Coaching Skills High/Low

Determine which CLEAR coaching skill—**C**hallenge, **L**isten, **E**ncourage, **A**sk, **R**efine—you are doing well at (highest score) and which two skills provide the most room for improvement.

Skill with highest score: _____

Skill with lowest score: _____

Skill with second-lowest score: _____

If you used Observer assessments with your CSI, use this section to record those scores and compare them to your self-assessment.

The *CSI: Self* and *CSI: Observer* are intended to be used as tools for self-evaluation for obtaining feedback from colleagues and co-workers. Grids are provided on the following pages for recording your CSI scores in each of the five categories:

- Coach

- Mentor

- Instructor

- Manager

- CLEAR coaching skills

For each grid on the following pages, record your self-ratings from your assessment in the *Self* column, then *sum total* your scores to obtain a total score at the bottom of that column. *Pay close attention to the statement numbers, as they are not always sequential.*

Following the same pattern, record each of the observer ratings in the subsequent seven columns. The grids are set up for up to seven observers, labeled A through G. Each number corresponds to a different observer. Total each observer column to find a total score for each observer.

ROLES

COACH								
Statement	Self	Observers' Ratings						
		A	B	C	D	E	F	G
1								
2								
3								
4								
5								
6								
7								
8								
9								
10								
Total								

MENTOR								
Statement	Self	Observers' Ratings						
		A	B	C	D	E	F	G
15								
16								
17								
18								
19								
20								
21								
22								
23								
24								
Total								

INSTRUCTOR								
Statement	Self	Observers' Ratings						
		A	B	C	D	E	F	G
25								
26								
27								
28								
29								
30								
31								
32								
33								
34								
Total								

MANAGER								
Statement	Self	Observers' Ratings						
		A	B	C	D	E	F	G
39								
40								
41								
42								
43								
44								
45								
46								
47								
48								
Total								

CLEAR COACHING SKILLS

CHALLENGE								
Statement	Self	Observers' Ratings						
		A	B	C	D	E	F	G
11								
12								
Total								

LISTEN								
Statement	Self	Observers' Ratings						
		A	B	C	D	E	F	G
13								
14								
Total								

ENCOURAGE								
Statement	Self	Observers' Ratings						
		A	B	C	D	E	F	G
35								
36								
Total								

ASK								
Statement	Self	Observers' Ratings						
		A	B	C	D	E	F	G
37								
38								
Total								

REFINE								
Statement	*Self*	*Observers' Ratings*						
		A	B	C	D	E	F	G
49								
50								
Total								

In reviewing the totals for each role and skill, the observer scores will provide you with feedback as to how others perceive you compared with your self-perceptions. If your self-score is in line with the observer scores, you probably have an accurate picture of yourself. If you find that the observer scores are higher than your own, then you probably exhibit certain behaviors more than you realize. If the observer scores are lower than your own, then you likely use certain behaviors less frequently than you realize.

Assuming all feedback is true, consider the following:

- What actions/behaviors are currently working for you?

- What actions/behaviors are not working for you?

- How will you manage your actions and behaviors differently so that others see you as you want to be portrayed?

- What role do others see you in most often compared with the role you see yourself in?

- Is there a disconnect in your CLEAR Coaching Skills scores?

- What CLEAR Coaching Skills do your observers indicate you are good at? Which do they think you need to work on?

Interpreting Your CSI Scores

The CSI provides clarification of which role you gravitate toward—*coach, manager, instructor,* or *mentor*—and the behaviors you exhibit most frequently, which are based on the application of specific coaching skills.

All four roles have their place and provide value based on the type of interaction and needs of the conversation at hand. The goal is not to eliminate any of these roles or even lessen them, but rather to increase your awareness of the shift that needs to occur as you transition from *manager, instructor,* or *mentor* into the role of *coach role.*

Identify the role you gravitate toward most (your highest score) so that you can identify more specifically where you want to focus as you make the shift to coach.

Understanding Your Scores

The *Roles* scores indicate your preferred or natural tendency and give you a basis for identifying trends in the roles you play most often. The *CLEAR Coaching Skills High/ Low* scores are intended to identify the skill you are most proficient at and the skill or skills that provide the greatest opportunity for improvement. The *Coaching Gap* score helps to illustrate the ease with which you can make the shift to the coach role.

Because everyone plays each of the four roles at one time or another, you may have any of the following outcomes in terms of your *Roles* scoring:

- Most people have one role score higher than all the rest; this means you have the tendency to gravitate toward that role most often or that you are most comfortable in that role. If this score is really high and the others are much lower, this could indicate that you may have a more difficult time flexing to or operating in the other roles.

- Many people have two high or equal role scores; this means that they can move in and out of those two roles easily, while the other two lower-scored roles are not likely to be used as often or with the same degree of comfort.

- Some people have three high or equal role scores; although this is less common, people with three high scores usually demonstrate a fair amount of flexibility in being able to take on the right role at the right time. The lowest score will still be the hardest role to move into.

- A few people will have high or equal scores in all four roles. If you have high scores in all four, congratulations! You are likely to have a tremendous amount of flexibility in using all the roles. You may also have an easier time determining what role to use in a given situation.

There are no "bad" roles. Some roles work better than others in certain situations, which is why it is important to learn how to flex to the right role based on the situation and the interaction. Although all roles are important and have their place, the goal here is to make you consciously competent in working within the *coach role*. In other words, do you know specifically what makes a good coach and when to coach? To better understand the *coach role*, it is helpful to understand the roles of *manager, mentor,* and *instructor* first.

Understanding Manager, Mentor, and Instructor

The distinctions among the four roles can best be explained by using the concept of "*what* and *how*," as shown below.

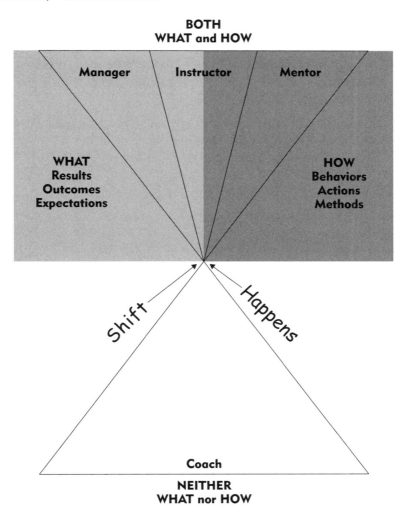

Conversations occur for any variety of reasons. Most conversations include *what* and *how*. One person communicates to the other person the *what*. **What is defined as the results, outcomes, goals, or objectives expected of the other person.** For example, a customer service group may have a target of returning 98 percent of customer voice-mails within twenty-four hours.

How is defined as the behaviors and actions (actionable items) that a person takes to achieve the what. For example, using the same customer service group example, the *how* for one person may be checking his voicemail between each call, making notes, and then returning all calls at the end of the day. Another customer service representative may use a different approach.

In this section, we review how the *what* and *how* are handled in each of three roles: *manager*, *mentor*, and *instructor*. The *coach role* will be covered in a subsequent section.

Manager Role

The *manager role* is not just a job title or position; anyone can play the manager role. The manager role is executed when the *what* of the task, project, or event is communicated to others. An example of a non-manager playing the manager role is when an employee takes responsibility for organizing a company picnic. The person will manage *what* needs to be accomplished and rely on others to carry out the *how*.

Great managers provide the *what* to others and allow the others autonomy to figure out *how* to get it done. For example, a sales manager may provide *what* needs to happen by providing a target: "We need to hit 90 percent of our sales goals by September." Then, the manager encourages employees, trusts their expertise, and lets them figure out *how* to make the 90 percent happen.

A manager . . .

- Identifies expectations, standards, processes, and results, and holds employees accountable to them.
- Allows autonomy in achieving results.
- Creates an environment in which employees are allowed to make mistakes and learn from them.
- Encourages innovation.
- Is flexible and open to new ideas.
- Encourages employees to expand on existing skills and build on strengths.
- Allows employees to figure out how to be successful and supports their efforts.
- Helps employees figure out how to resolve performance deficits.
- Supports behaviors or actions that lead to improved interactions with team members and greater productivity.

Mentor Role

Mentors provide the *how*, not the *what*. The *what* is provided by the person seeking the mentor's expertise. For example, if a person being coached wants to know *what* he or she needs to do to get noticed within the company, he or she would approach the mentor seeking information on *how* to make it happen. In this situation, the mentor might say something like the following, "If you really want the senior staff to notice you, get in front of them more often by volunteering to do the monthly budget presentation."

A mentor . . .

- Provides advice and support to a person who is interested in career planning or advancement.

- Helps develop a person's political savvy and sensitivity to organizational culture and environment.

- Provides persons with proactive approaches for managing their own careers.

- Suggests an educational course of action or provides information and resources for professional development.

- Tells people how to prepare so that one day they can move into the mentor's job.

Instructor Role

An instructor provides people with both the *what* and the *how*. Providing both the *what and* the *how* is often used by instructors to teach people new skills, and by consultants who are hired to provide both the *what* and the *how* from an expert perspective. Instructors provide both *what* and *how* by way of teaching, training, tutoring, consulting, and presenting.

An instructor . . .

- Provides knowledge to help someone become proficient.

- Teaches skills that make others successful.

- Provides instruction to new or less experienced persons.

- Presents information, processes, or steps to perform a task.

- Provides "expert" advice on what to do and how to do it.

Shift Happens! Letting Go of What and How

When operating as coach, you must make a conscious shift to the *coach role* and solicit answers from the person being coached (PBC). The first step is to let go of the *what* and the *how*. When you let go of both the *what* and the *how*, you enter the world of coaching. It is at this precise point at which you change your thinking from being the one to provide answers and solutions to being the one who draws *all* of the answers and solutions from the PBC. In essence, you become *egoless* (without ego or bias), deriving your satisfaction from making others the experts and helping them achieve success through coaching, rather than being successful by fixing, doing, or being the expert.

What happens once you make the shift to coach will be amazing!

Coach Role

Coaching can be a mental challenge as you learn that you are no longer in control of, or providing, the *what* or the *how*. This concept is difficult to grasp for most people because they have been known, rewarded, promoted, and encouraged for being the ones with all the answers (the experts). Most of us take pride in providing direction, guidance, solutions, explanations, and ideas. Put plain and simply, many of us just can't help ourselves from wanting to fill in all the blanks. In fact, we usually see that behavior as "helpful."

As you transition to the *coach role,* you will learn that the coach provides neither the *what* nor the *how* to the PBC. You may ask, "How is this possible?" Think of this in terms of what role each person plays in a coaching conversation. It's not that the *what* and *how* are completely absent from the coaching conversation, it's just that the PBC *owns* both of them, not you.

Although either person (coach or PBC) can begin any coaching conversation, the concept of the coach releasing control of the *what* and *how* is certainly *more* obvious when the PBC communicates the *why* of the conversation (*Why* are we having this coaching conversation?) to the coach. This typically occurs at the very beginning of the conversation. The PBC then communicate *what* he or she wants to have happen. It is then the coach's job to skillfully draw out of the PBC *how* to make it happen.

There are times when the coach will be the one communicating the *why* (*Why* are we having this coaching conversation?) to the PBC. This situation most often occurs with performance coaching conversations. During performance coaching, the coach gives the *why* and then works to get the PBC to take ownership so that the PBC can own the *what* and the *how.*

Examples:

PBC communicates WHY: "I've been meaning to talk with you. I'm working on improving my partnering ability and ran into something that I need help with."

In this example, you should help the PBC determine *how* he will improve his partnering ability and overcome this obstacle. If you launch into telling this person *how* to fix the problem, you have taken on the *mentor role,* not the *coach role.*

Coach communicates WHY: "I've noticed that you're not that comfortable in front of an audience, yet your role requires that you present information frequently. I know that you want to be successful in this area. How do you think you can become more comfortable presenting?"

Here you can see that the coach is not taking responsibility for what will happen or how it will occur.

A coach . . .

- Uses a coaching process to help the PBC gain insight and move forward.

- Challenges the PBC's status quo.

- Listens more than talks.

- Encourages the PBC to take risks.

- Encourages PBCs to find their own solutions.

- Asks more than tells.

- Remains *egoless* and sets bias aside.

- Provides opportunities for exploration of new ideas.
- Provides clarity to the coaching conversation.

When to Coach

The *coach role* is best used for interactions that move the PBC forward, specifically when the PBC:

- Needs insight about his or her behavior and actions.
- Is feeling stagnant, stuck, or has outgrown a role.
- Has a drive for greatness.
- Is not sure what is interfering with the ability to achieve some personal or professional goal.
- Needs to find a way to move forward or make progress.
- Is trying to move from average or good to better and best.
- Realizes that some technical, organizational, or other problem is blocking his or her performance or potential.
- Has a very difficult choice to make, such as the decision to take on a new role or new challenge.
- Needs help preparing for an upcoming difficult conversation or presentation.

The coach's role is to help the PBC gain insight and understanding regarding the topic of conversation, not to solve the problem for him or her. In coaching conversations, the coach spends the majority of time (about 80 percent) listening and the remaining time (about 20 percent) asking mostly open-ended coaching questions. Many coaches struggle with not solving, or want to direct the conversation to their end. Coaching is often the role that people think they are in, when in reality they are more likely in one of the other roles (manager, mentor, or instructor). This is a common "ah-ha" that people have when taking this inventory.

Who Should Coach?

Coaching is not just a stand-alone profession. It can and should be used by anyone who interacts with people. Coaching can and should be a part of everybody's job! People who have assigned leadership roles should strive to become proficient in the coach role. Managers, when not playing the manager role, should know how to coach. People in every organization and in every position should have the opportunity to learn how to be coaches. Coaching does not depend on one's having a certain organizational position or title. It depends on having the desire to help others succeed and possessing the knowledge and skills that it takes to work through the process of a coaching conversation.

Becoming a Skillful Coach

You already determined which of the five CLEAR coaching skills is your strongest, based on your highest score, and which skill(s) needs improvement, based on your lowest score. The following information will give you a brief overview of the CLEAR coaching skills and provide a starting point for your development.

CLEAR Coaching Skills

<u>C</u>hallenge

<u>L</u>isten

<u>E</u>ncourage

<u>A</u>sk

<u>R</u>efine

CLEAR coaching skills are used to aid the success of the entire coaching conversation.

Challenge   All of the techniques used to present the PBC with a meaningful Challenge are challenging themselves. Challenging because they ask the coach to be diligent, present in the moment, and willing to challenge the PBC's status quo.

Challenge is about helping the PBC experience an ah-ha moment or a shift in his or her own thinking. It is used when a PBC is stuck and needs a little push or when a PBC requires feedback regarding incongruence or a disconnect in his or her behaviors or comments. The purpose of Challenge is to provide PBCs with insight that will help them move forward or away from an impending disaster.

Challenge includes:

- Reality checks—truthful statements intended to make PBCs aware of blind spots.
- Requests—assignments that stretch PBCs.

Listen   When in the coach role, it is important to Listen to more than just the words being said. This requires you to be diligent in talking less and paying close attention to non-verbal clues, both in face-to-face interactions and virtually. During the coaching conversation, listen for what *is not* said as much as for what *is* said. Coaches who Listen display the following behaviors:

- They are present and focused on the PBC.
- They show respect in their own verbal and non-verbal dialog.
- They let PBCs know they are being heard and understood.
- They don't multitask (turn off monitors/computers/cell phones, forward the phone, and do not do email while virtual coaching).
- They don't make assumptions.

Coaches hear main ideas, key points, changes in tone, and unnatural pauses and are able to ascertain strengths, values, wants, and needs of the PBC.

Coaches Listen without evaluating by making sure that they understand a question before they try to answer it and by not forcing a problem into their own frames of reference (*coaching biases*). The coach does not decide if what the PBC says is right or wrong, workable or not, it just is.

Coaches Listen during all stages of a conversation in order to understand. One caution about listening is that you must be disciplined in not creating blocks to the free and easy development of a mutual interaction. It is easy to stop listening when you hear something you disagree with and even easier to stop listening as soon as you think you know how to fix a problem for the PBC.

Good listeners, when in the *coach role,* encourage story telling from the PBC and understand the benefits, of silence during coaching conversations.

Encourage Encourage is all about making PBCs feel good about themselves and recognizing their emotions, feelings, and accomplishments. It is about moving people forward and about giving them reasons to continue to make progress toward their goals. It is an essential part of coaching because it validates feelings and emotions and enhances esteem and confidence.

Encourage can be accomplished by making statements that:

- Validate PBCs' feelings and emotions.
- Celebrate PBCs' accomplishments.

The Encourage skill builds on other skills by making the coaching conversation personal and individualized. It is the job of the coach to validate PBCs' emotions and feelings as well as keep them on the right track, moving forward appropriately and succeeding. As much as coaches play the role of truth-sayer or reality-check person and occasionally devil's advocate, in many ways, coaches also are PBCs' biggest cheerleaders and supporters. In the case of executive or senior-level leaders, the coach may be one of the few people who provide recognition and encouragement.

Ask Ask the PBC coaching questions. How?

- Ask open-ended, powerful, and thought-provoking questions that start with what and how.
- Ask based on what was said, not what you think you heard.
- Ask based on the person's needs, not yours.
- Ask with a powerful statement (Tell me more . . .).

Refine Keep the coaching conversation and the PBC on track, focused, and moving forward.

- Encourage personal accountability on the part of the PBC.
- Eliminate blame from either side.
- Break complex topics into manageable chunks.
- Keep the conversation focused on the PBC's contributions and accountabilities.

- Use techniques such as metaphors and Two-Words to focus the PBC.

- Additional Refine techniques can be found in *Coaching for Commitment: Achieving Superior Performance from Individuals on Teams* (3rd ed.).

Questions to Think About

What percent of time do you spend in each role?

Coach _____ percent

Manager _____ percent

Instructor _____ percent

Mentor _____ percent

How do you use the various roles in your job?

_____

_____

_____

_____

_____

_____

_____

_____

_____

_____

_____

In what situations are you currently using another role that would be better suited to using the *coach role*?

_____

_____

_____

_____

_____

_____

_____

_____

_____

_____

_____

How conscious are you about what role you are operating from when interacting with others (*coach, manager, instructor,* and *mentor*)?

_____

_____

_____

_____

_____

_____

_____

_____

_____

What observations can you make about your CLEAR coaching skills scores?

_____

_____

_____

_____

_____

_____

_____

_____

_____

_____

_____

_____

_____

_____

_____

_____

_____

_____

For more information on coaching, the value proposition for coaching, what happens within the coach role, how to enhance your CLEAR coaching skills, and how to gain long-lasting commitment from the PBC, refer to the *Coaching for Commitment* book (3rd ed.) and its companion coaching training accompanying workshop.